G000123537

CONDENSATIONS OF SPIRITUAL WISDOM,

AND OTHER ESSAYS.

Written by Spirit and Transcribed
by

Brendan O'Callaghan

I.S.M. Publications

.

ISBN: 9798702048246

Cover design by: Brendan O'Callaghan

.

Dedicated to those who work tirelessly for God and the enlightenment of human consciousness.

.

"The greatest fear is ignorance.

The greatest gift is the release from fear.

Wisdom is that gift.

Reject and remain fearfully ignorant.

Accept and become truly free."

'Spirit'

INTRODUCTION.

Every so often a flash of inspiration enters my mind and I find a need to transcribe it immediately. Unfortunately, this is usually late at night or early morning. I call these inspirations "condensations". It seems that they appear on my mind and remind me of the steam from a kettle condensing on a mirror, the moisture appearing from nowhere.

Maybe that it is that somewhere in the world of matter a question has been raised. Spirit because it is spirit cannot give a direct answer to those who will not or cannot listen. Spirit then uses an available and usable channel to give its answer. The Spirit answer condenses on the mind of the medium, and in my situation, I write the answer down. The Word then is brought into our world.... the world of matter... and,." the Word is made flesh".

Another image I get from these words is that they contain more meaning then at first appears. They are condensed wisdom which when left to rest in the back of the mind expand and find application in the everyday life of the developing spirit incarnate. Please constantly question this wisdom until it becomes true to you. Please apply this wisdom to aid your spiritual growth. Above all look for God in your life and receive His answers to your questions, in whatever form is deemed most suitable to you. God Bless you in your quest.

Brendan O'Callaghan, the transcriber of these condensations.

CONTENTS.

CONTENTS contd

CONTENTS contd.

SPIRITUAL WISDOM

ABOUT RELIGION.

All religions have very violent histories. Mankind is still embroiled in religious war with no sign of solution.

THINGS JUST ARE.

At times we have difficulty in understanding how things should be but my experience is that they should always be as they are. What makes the difference good or bad is how we handle them. We are in the Light, working for the Light, providing no more than the opportunity for enlightenment. Others must take their responsibilities around that. We can take no responsibility for their decisions rather we pray that they will respond in a way that will in some way spread the Light. That is our hope, not our responsibility.

CRIME AND PUNISHMENT.

No crime deserves to be punished. The fact that a crime exists is an indication of the lack of personal education provided for the perpetrator by society. The crime can be seen as a backlash onto the society that held the perpetrator in ignorance, everybody is the victim.

GOD'S LAW.

God is subject to His own Laws including the Law of Cause and effect.

HAPPY TO BE ALIVE.

People find they are happy to be alive after near death. When they are dead, they are also happy to be still alive.

THE LINE BETWEEN THE GOOD AND BAD.

The line between the good and bad aspects of the human is finer than the finest hair. Watch the human struggle to decide which side they wish to be on. See them test the apparent advantages available to them in their quest for very often misperceived fulfilment. On the negative side of this fine line they express themselves as controllers of their fellow humans thus avoiding the opportunity to discover the folly of their ways by the reflection of opposition to their actions. They bully their way along the road of development, continuously controlling life and directing it to what they think is the correct goal. These people cannot be Divinely guided as their excursion into the greyness of negativity put them beyond the reach of true love and also leaves them vulnerable to greater negative influence, endorsing their misinterpretation of the correctness of their incorrect actions.

THE NOW.

The past is encapsulated in the present, as is the future, except that the future is only a potential not a fact until it becomes present. The now is always present and the nearest we can be to the future.

ILLNESS.

The worst thing that illness can do to you is kill you. Life is all about gathering awareness in preparation for the next phase of our spiritual development. This next phase will require a change in our make-up and most often requires that we shed our physical bodies, in other words our bodies must die. Therefore, all our life we are in preparation for the death process whether we are aware or not. If this is true then the worst that illness can do to you can inevitably be the best for you. Illness can provide you with the ticket home. Illness can also provide you with the means to reassess your sense of reality and permit you to carry on with your journey of development that will eventually end with your passing into your next phase on the infinite journey of spiritual development. Illness is always good, it's how it is used that shows the benefit or otherwise.

GOD.

There is only one God and to seek to encapsulate God in the simple form of a trinity is to attempt to introduce other forms of God that are only relevant to those who seek to exercise their control through religion over their "minions".

NOT GOD.

There is only one God but that God has so many facets, a personality and form that is the perception of every individual creature who looks to see God. If we could share our perceptions, we could get a greater, more complete understanding of the greatness and goodness that is God. Religions do not encourage this sharing rather they seek to impose their view of God and their view alone, presenting only the narrowest view, but one that gives the religion the control over another's spirituality. The individual following a religion has irresponsibly surrendered their Spirit to that belief.

Under these circumstances if an individual harbours guilt the aspect of God they will perceive will be as the God of truth and therefore a threatening judgemental God, and this is not God.

WISDOM.

Though we may be ignorant before and even during an event, it is always a hope that we will be wise after the event.

GOODNESS OF DISEASE.

What a great disease it is that rekindles God in man.

LIMITED INFINITY?

When we're dealing with things spiritual everything is infinite. All potentials constantly exist. What potential that is for you only exists within your capable perception, which is only limited by your awareness. It is vital to be aware of this limitation but also allow yourself to dream into a greater awareness using hypothesis and supposition.

A QUESTION.

Why does truth always need to be reached through hypothesis?

ANOTHER QUESTION.

Why does science need to prove what exists, exists, and if they can't prove its existence accept this un-provability as evidence of its non-existence?

AN EASTER THOUGHT.

Just a thought, Easter is a time of death and resurrection - for everyone. The symbolism of the chicken breaking from the confines of its shell is an inspiration to us to break from that which limits us and like the chicken begin living.

Happy Easter.

IN TRUTH, IT IS ALL GOOD.

Here's the hypothesis - there is no right or wrong, there's truth, untruth and non-truth. It could be said truth is right, untruth is ignorance and non-truth is wrong. But there is only truth, all else is imagined ignorance. The law of cause and effect rules the universe. All actions are subject to that law and all reactions are the effect of that law being enforced. Thus, it could also be hypothesised that all actions are correct under the law as are all reactions correct. It is the truth expressing itself. It is our experience that tells us how the effect has affected us and we tend to deem favourable affects good and adverse effects bad or right or wrong, where in truth it was all good.

A SACRED PLACE.

A Spiritual Centre is God's place and that one's input into the centre is to service the physical side and to be a channel for God. As in healing etc. the channel is important and sacred, so with the Centre, the channel provided by those who work in the Centre is important and sacred.

ABOUT LOVE.

Love is almost eternally elusive. How can you find
what you do not understand? Most certainly the
only way is through following the spiritual path
back to God. God is love, beyond our
comprehension, beyond our imagination. As we
increase our understanding of God, so we
increasingly understand love. We increasingly
become aware of how we feel love. As our
spiritual awareness develops, so does our
sensitivity to those love feelings. We begin to feel
God within our being, that being that is part of
God. And our relationship with our God-self
deepens taking us closer to our evolving
destination, unity within God, deeply in love.

31

A SATIRICAL VIEW OF ST. PATRICK.

Patrick caused serious eco damage - he got rid of a complete indigenous species - snakes. Patrick damaged property - he lit bonfires, knocked over standing stones, desecrated sacred sites and stabbed the King in the foot. The arrival of Patrick heralded the subjugation of Ireland by Rome. Patrick attacked the Spirit of Ireland and beat it into the past. Is it therefore surprising that the day dedicated to him is a day of excessive eating and drinking and debauchery? It could be said that Patrick was Irelands first gurrier*.

(*'gurrier' is Irish slang for an unruly young man.)

LIGHT OR DARK?

The future can be light or dark for us depending on our decisions. If we choose the dark then cause and effect comes into play, out of the necessity to learn, and we can make the darkness light. Inevitably all there is, is light. Focus on that future and the present will enable you to achieve it.

MEMORIES.

Memories continue to exist in an elemental form, an energy image sustained by the energy of the incarnate participants of the original event, who feed the memory through their positive or negative impressions and how these impressions continue to exercise the consciousness of those involved, good memories or bad ones. These memories will also continue to exist after the participants demise fed by the energy of the descendants of those involved, in how the event continues to affect the lives of the successors.

THE FUTURE.

There is no future, except for what you create today.

ANALYSE THIS.

To the analytical mind simplicity is complex.

SOUL.

The Soul, is the over-rated being,

TIME.

There are two types of time in this world, God time and Man-time. Humankind in general lives by Man-time. The exception are the indigenous people, they still live by God time. I remember as a child watching the farmers going about their business and every now and then they would look to see where the sun was in the heavens, this was God time

'SPIRITUALIST'S' WORLD.

God does not lie, and as Spirit is of God, neither can a Spirit lie nor mislead. The world that many 'Spiritualists' call the Spirit world is not in fact purely Spirit but a multitude of 'levels' of consciousness.

ON SPIRIT COMMUNICATION.

If we can learn to smile rather than grimace, we give our Spirit a chance to evoke the Law of Cause and effect. Many who call themselves spiritual or spiritualist are only psychic and not spiritual, at all, and those they communicate with, or defer to, are stuck in, or have to come 'down' to, a soul level in order to come within the consciousness of the so called 'Spiritualist'. Any psychic can contact soul but only a Spirit can contact Spirit. It is the Spirit of the medium and not the medium themselves that does the God work. The Spirit cannot do this unless the medium is spiritually aware.

SOUL STATE.

In the state of soul, we can find that ignorance co-exists with wisdom. When a medium connects into the soul consciousness is when strong discernment is required. Unfortunately, religion has made many unaware of the difference between soul and Spirit states, as has spiritualism become a religion and confused us regarding the difference between psychic and spiritual. We now refer to bad or evil Spirits whereas we are only talking about ignorant souls, often no more evolved than the mediums they employ.

QUESTION OR ANSWER.

Which is more important, the question or the answer? How many ask a question just to find out if others have an answer or if their answer is the same? How many question, just for the sake of asking? How many ask a question to divert from the subject under discussion? How many answer, to impose their authority or opinion? How many answer a different question than that asked? How many answer a question with a question? How many answer? See how many questions I've just asked? I don't need an answer to any of them. I'm sure these questions have created further questions in your mind. I'll end this point by asking again, which is more important, the question or the answer?

ARTIFICIAL INTELLIGENCE.

AI, (artificial intelligence), is only as smart as those humans who develop it. Spirituality is smarter as it is developed by Spirit, (God). God looks after itself. If you can recognise you are part of God, God will look after you.

SPIRITUAL HEALING.

The difference between Spiritual Healing and all other energy healing forms is that Spiritual Healing is through the love of God and all other comes from the love of the human. It is only Spiritual Healing when it's called Spiritual Healing and it is unconditional. If it carries another name then it is never Spiritual Healing and doesn't come from God.

DEATH-RIGHT.

We come into this world on a two-way (return) ticket. All use the one way to get here, birth, and though we all eventually use death to return home we all make our individual choices of travel arrangements. Some choose illness, some choose 'accident', some choose suicide, some choose old age. Whatever your choice is its always right for you.

THE OPPORTUNITY OF ILLNESS.

Illness is always an opportunity and never an excuse. As an opportunity it can help you change your life, as an excuse it can kill you.

TRUTH.

We can believe something to be true but it might or might not be so. At best belief can be used to access the question of truthfulness, but can never replace truth. It is true when you can say you know it to be true. Belief resides in the ego mind, truth in the spiritual mind. I have noticed that when a statement that is made, especially what turns out to be a true statement, and offers an alternative to the belief of the believer, the believer becomes defensive in order to support their beliefs, whereas the truth sayer will always ponder the alternatives offered, without taking offence, or feeling threatened. Truth is also dynamic and personal, and belief is fixed and accepted by many without adequate questioning. Because it is dynamic truth always is now, belief can extend from the past to the future. I think I'll stick to the truth.

GOD?

Have you ever considered that God might be a 'what' rather than a 'who'. Try asking the question 'what is God', instead of 'who is God'. This will give the way for a new understanding of God. What is God? God is a spirit. This answer gives us a fresh range of questions such as 'what is a spirit'? This line of questioning allows us to deviate from the popular imagery of God, the supreme in human form, typically depicted in Michael Angelo's statue, and away from the idea of a spirit as a ghostly form though still in a human shape, and then to a notion of pure energy. What is pure energy? God, a what!

THE MESSENGER.

The message is more important than the messenger. In religion the messenger is deified and the message misquoted and modified to suit the politics of the time.

UNAWARE.

Everybody contains a beautiful Spirit but sometimes the body misbehaves. No one is their behaviour though we often rush to judge them by it. Nobody is bad, only unaware.

LOVE.

Love flows through the Divine nature of every being whether it is in the form of animal, including human animal, or tree or even stone. It cannot flow through the ego. All love is unconditional. If there is a condition it is not love.

SUCCESSFULLY FAIL.

An optimistic pessimist sees failure as success.

GENDER.

Women only show their weakness when they try to be strong like men instead of strong like women and men visa versa. When we utilise our natural abilities and strengths we work and live within our gender and the energy of that gender; woman with feminine energy and a man with masculine energy. We can never be happy any other way.

HOMOSEXUALITY.

Homosexuality has its place in every society provided it is also utilised as a true function of our being. There are situations where we can have a body of a particular gender but energised by the energy of the opposite gender. This, because it is a selection of the Spirit, is natural but also presents a uniqueness that plays a vital role in life. Unfortunately, in certain societies this is seen as an unnatural "condition" whereas in other societies it is revered. The former is so wrong. If someone is born this way how can it be unnatural? Cannot it be a blessing that we should have this uniqueness? This means we can then have a man with the feminine sensitivities of a woman and a woman with the masculine strengths of a man.

DISABILITY?

Downs Syndrome was treated as a condition that had to be treated by locking the afflicted into institutions where those children were treated in an unkindly and unnatural way. It is only recently that we have become aware that they are the epitome of a spiritual being offering unconditional love. There are other conditions that also respond so well when we recognise that the condition allows such expression, but unfortunately, we reject this expression and see it only as a symptom of this condition that society deems unnatural.

AUTISM?

Autism also is considered unnatural. Cannot it just be a natural response to unnatural circumstances?

A child acting out of some predetermined character, a character that society has determined. An Autistic child demands particular attention but so often we determine what attention should be given and so often medicate.

UNIQUE PEOPLE.

There are many other conditions that are labelled as disabilities but as we are born with them, they cannot be classified as abnormal. They could be called special conditions as they require what is called normal to treat them uniquely. The disability appears in the inability of those labelled normal being unable to allow this uniqueness to be correctly utilised by the unique person and by society. It is the inability of so called normal to embrace the gift of this uniqueness that could earn normal the label of disabled. We try to fix what isn't broken and to change the uniqueness into normality or as close as we can get to that.

DIFFERENTLY-ABLED.

We have seen certain conditions, that are becoming more common these days, causing great difficulties within family units as the family struggles to cope with the disruption of the apparent illness or disability. This is classified as a problem whereas it could be looked on as an opportunity for humankind to adapt to a new understanding as to why it is necessary for these conditions to manifest. The tendency is to treat the condition as a disability rather than differently abled.

THE NECESSARY CHANGE.

When we see another behaving in a manner that is not considered normal why can we not treat this situation as a whole new experience for us to learn by, not try to treat the condition with the hope that we may cure it and bring the "sufferer" into our normal world to behave normally. This does not just refer to mental conditions but to physical conditions also. We have created a world around our capabilities to the exclusion of exceptional or unique situations. It is only in recent times that we have made pedestrian road crossings usable by the visually impaired, that we have made public places and public transport wheelchair friendly, that we have included facilities in schools for special needs, that we have begun to language these differences in a kinder and understanding way. However, we still treat these uniquely-abled as disabled.

AS GOD CREATED.

This is a wonderful place that God has created for us all, both common and unique. Humankind has created an unfriendly world that has little facility to accommodate any variation in human characteristics. Interestingly this does not apply to all humankind but particularly to what could be called White Caucasian society, the society that has gone out into the world to colonise and conquer others, the society that has sought to impose its religious beliefs on others, a society that has sought to enslave others and to enslave those of its own society that were "different", a society that removed spirituality and replaced it with religion.

LIFE PURPOSE.

If we are to realise the purpose of life, we need to understand who we are. We were not born a Christian but were born into a Christian family, a Christian society. We are not naturally Christian. Humankind devised religion and society adapted it to control members of that society. We are an aspect of God, we are Spirit. The physical being cannot exist without its Spirit. We cannot be born into life, with life, unless we have that essential ingredient, Spirit. Everything is imbued with the spirit of its creator and its creator is imbued with the Spirit of The Creator, God.

JUST DIFFERENT PEOPLE.

When next we encounter a situation or person that is different than us let us see them as unique and a gift to us to help us realise that there is nothing good or bad, nothing right or wrong but that there are differences. Let us not label those differences so that we can lock them out of our lives. Let us embrace those differences, they help life to be so interesting and those that are different have so much to teach us. God loves them, why can't we love them and their uniqueness?

AND OTHER ESSAYS.

Condensations of Spiritual Wisdom.

MEMORIES.

Memories are often misused and misunderstood. Memories have a purpose other than the idle meanderings of part of the human mind. Memories can also be the useful recall of the spiritual mind; they can be your "Guardian Angel", your "higher self" guiding your ego. But this can only happen with permission from your ego. As God does not interfere in your life, neither can your higher self, your Spirit. In the hypothesis that we have free will, we normally accept that this licence extends to our ego, whereas in fact it stops with our Spirit. Our ego takes it as its right also, because that's what egoism does. This is where memories come in and remind us that this is not the case. Too often we choose to ignore them or select the negative ones to preoccupy our thoughts. This is the domain of the subconscious controlling the life of the subject it is seeking to have power over.

Memories can generate feelings and emotions and bring them to the surface in a pleasant or unpleasant manner. It is important when these emotions arise that we seek to evaluate them so that we can benefit positively from them. If we don't there is a likely hood that we will suppress them and feed into the negative side of our existence, our negative ego side. We accept that an ego is a necessary part of every human being but it does need to be recognised and controlled, if not it will take over our lives and push out what it considers its rival, our benign Spirit. As our Spirit is of God it makes, like God, no demands on the human form it occupies. Our Spirit is there for the journey this body can take it on, an adventure into wonderland. Every journey has spiritual purpose, whether the ego knows it or not, but cannot be evaluated in spiritual terms as long as the ego is in control, and this is where the memory fits in. Every life event is experienced on at least two levels, the spiritual level and the ego level. No doubt you will want to know about the other levels other than the two we mention, but then that is your ego being inquisitive or disrupting your train of thought. At an ego level it will be categorised as a good or bad event, whereas at a spiritual level it will only ever be a good experience. In the former situation, where the ego evaluates the experience should it be considered a bad experience, the ego will seek to mitigate the experience by blaming and avoiding any responsibility for the event and thus lose any benefit that can accrue from the scenario of what has just occurred. This is the usual response of the ego when pain in any form is felt around circumstances that the ego has led its human form into. In these circumstances the memory of the event is suppressed and hidden away. However, it is never so far away that it doesn't continue to play a part in our lives while it is resident in our subconscious. By our resurrecting this memory, through our preparedness to spiritually re-evaluate it, we can turn it around and remove it from our subconscious and bring it into consciousness beneficially.

If we can embrace the hypothesis that bad things happen for good reasons then we can go a long way towards a better life, both spiritually and egotistically. This can only be done through the positive use of memory. As we have said memories can

66

generate feelings and emotions, sad emotions and happy emotions. As was also said many times before, a simple spiritual rule of thumb, "If it makes you happy do it, if it doesn't then don't do it". Before making a decision ask yourself the question "am I happy about this, will this make me happy?" And if you feel it will, then find out by doing it. Remember you always have the right to change your mind. It is only those who seek to control you that would seek to make you stick with your first choice and thus continuously subject you to this unhappiness you have found through the incorrect decision, for you, that you have made. No contract should be binding; every contract should have a "get out" clause. God gave us happiness as well as unhappiness so that we can tell the difference between good and bad decisions. Why then do we continue to so willingly accept unhappiness? Because our ego will never accept the responsibility of only seeking to do what makes it truly happy. Being truly happy is where our Spirit is contented. The ego is always prepared to suffer for what it sees as its goals in life. A spiritually ignorant ego has no idea of what that goal is, doesn't understand the true purpose of life and yet is measuring its choices, often at best, under the guidance of its perceived religion. We have said before how religion is created by humankind and for its means of controlling the human population through the misuse of spiritual principles modified to suit the society that creates it. Those in "power" in that society depend on the population of that society for the power they have and will promise anything to achieve that position. Once they get into that powerful position, they will invariably forget those promises, but the memory has stored them so they will always be there to haunt them until they can purge them.

Memories can be carried over into the next life also and can continue to haunt the soul, that part of the ego that survives physical death. This is that soul's purgatory, the irresponsible "woe is me" state, unable to take responsibility for putting itself in that position. Often the pain of that soul can be felt back into the physical world, particularly by those whose lives have been affected by this soul. Again, we must remember that this pain is felt in our memory. We can help this unfortunate soul. Forgiveness never works but understanding can. This understanding can be gained by opening to the hypothesis that this person whose soul is unhappy played such an important part in our life, and indeed was in our life as a consequence of choices we have made, along with choices they made, and were there for a good reason, even if only to highlight the good or bad significance of our choices. We must bear no malice towards the subject of these memories with this soul. Our understanding, no matter how basic, will present the opportunity of love to enter the evaluation. The arrival of appreciation for the lesson gained from the experience, will introduce love and healing of the negativity, and will instantly become part of the process of redemption, in both worlds, this physical world and in the soul world. The demented will no more in pain and their Spirit will be released from its now used and bruised ego. So, memories are more than the meandering of the physical mind. It's a treasure trove of happiness and healing. Remember this.

CANCER.

Cancer, the diagnosis that opens everybody to fear and places us into the hands of doctors and quacks, who are also governed by the same fear as the cancer sufferer. There is only one cure for cancer and that is a change of attitude, not only within the mind of the "victim' or target of the negativity causing the 'illness', but also a change in the attitude in the minds of all who are drawn into the circle of fear. The target is selected by the negativity when it has the seed thought of their fear of the illness and is triggered by the need of the 'victim' to eradicate that fear, and the illness itself is Spirit given for that purpose. The negativity we talk of is that negativity that lies within the ego of the 'victim' and is seeking to control the spiritual purpose of the journey of the Spirit that is embodied in that ego. It needs to be recognised that the ego itself is the victim and bears all the suffering, both physical and mental, from the illness and from any subsequent treatments deemed appropriate by the well-meaning health practitioner, but they are often uninitiated though medically qualified, or by equally uninitiated "alternative health" practitioners, also equally qualified but through their official bodies, for their fears and unawareness. Hence, the use of the word 'victim' for the target of this, now collective, negativity. The ego is the target as it is its own negativity that draws the need for this particular illness and often raises the question by the diagnosis of "why me". There is a saying, "Everyone eventually reaches the level of their own incompetence", and in this case of course refers to the ego's own limitations. Because of the ego thinking that this world it occupies infers particular rights upon its existence, and this life is there to serve it, it is a huge revelation to the ego to realise that this is possibly not the case. The ego cannot accept this and then begins the process of denial, excuses, blame and reaction. A word, obvious by its omission is REALISATION.

Realisation comes through awareness and awareness is one's own Spirit talking to the ego. Those who are engrossed in the ego are the victims in this scenario as they will find it the most difficult to accept spiritual realisation, and require the ultimate confrontation with the threat of the demise of the ego, without the reassurance of any future beyond this life. It is unfortunate that the only resource that is offered to the 'sufferer' is the offer presented by so-called modern medicine. It is, however, important that we do not discard this facility as it also has its place if utilised correctly. The unfortunate aspect of this treatment is the mistreatment or misuse of this treatment by the profession that governs it. The background to the real treatment of disease that is no longer recognised is the spiritual quotient, the real treatment, and is the reason why Spiritual Healing is the most effective modality in the area of energy healing. All other energy healing, no matter how they may be dressed up by the practitioners, or by the philosophy, can be compared to Spiritual Healing unless it is practiced as such. Spiritual Healing in order to be effective requires that those practising it have sound spiritual awareness. Spiritual awareness serves all of life's ills and every spiritually aware person is therefore a Spiritual Healer. Spiritual awareness is not a module in any medical school or course involving modern medicine, and indeed in most, if not all, energy healing courses. It is often asked how can a true Spiritual Healer be recognised and the simple answer is that as all have the capacity to be a channel for God, the Spirit, then those who's ego allows them to recognise their own Spirit, the Spirit within, can inspire the dis-eased back to a healthier attitude and to no longer need the illness they have experienced, and at times to be able to release their dominant and illness creating ego altogether. This latter situation being that their Spirit and soul can enter the next stage of its evolvement. Whatever the outcome of a true Spiritual Healing treatments with a true Spiritual Healer there will always be a greater sense of peace and assurance that exceeds any expectation that the 'sufferer' might have. This sense cannot be associated with the actual physical or conversational interaction between the 'patient' and the 'practitioner' and can only be associated with some other source, that source being the Divine Source known as God; not the universe or any of the myriad terms used within many energy healing methods to account for their apparent 'powers', and to feed the egos of the practitioners and the egos of their 'victims'.

A true Spiritual Healer will never target the illness but will work at the behest of The Spirit, channelling unconditionally God's love to the confused or ignorant ego of the sufferer, thus empowering them spiritually in their lives and enabling their Spirit to take over and guide the ego along the path that had originally been envisaged prior to this incarnation. It can often be found that the delay in this redirection had created within the physical body a disharmony that medicine called cancer. This cancer often requires medical intervention in order to remove the 'infection' that is physically manifesting but will not deal with the continuous cause unless it is accompanied by Spiritual Awareness. Spiritual awareness always removes the cause. Unfortunately, too much responsibility is given to medical science to treat spiritual dysfunctions and this is why so often medical intervention fails. It can be noted how cancer invariably introduces the sufferer to a different regime in lifestyle and living, mainly due to the debilitating effect and hopelessness it instils in its victim, so often with the help of the medical doctor assigned to this case, one with little or no spiritual awareness.

Religious knowledge is of little use as it usually infers that the illness is but a punishment for past or current deeds and guilty conscience further compounds the dilemma. The change of lifestyle and living is the catalyst for remission from all illness but must be accompanied by spiritual awareness. In spiritual terms this remission is really the opportunity to return to the original purpose of this incarnation, a spiritual journey. Unfortunately, this re-mission restores the ex-sufferer to a state in life when they, like so many addicts, yearn to return to what they once perceived as normality, thus leaving their re-mission and reverting instead to their old mission that caused them to have the illness in the first place, and this makes their illness terminal. In order to ensure that his reversion does not occur the re-mitted will require the continued support of a spiritually aware person but only until such time as their own awareness can be maintained and their own inspiration recognised by themselves.

So, we see how fear-based illness is and especially that illness known as cancer. Cancer needs this respect as other illnesses do not carry the message that the afflicted requires in order for them to heed it. It is a pity that Spirit needs to go to such lengths to draw a person's attention to their dysfunctional life and lifestyle. It's a greater pity that the person has moved so far from spiritual awareness that they do not even have the awareness of this distance they have come from the simple truth that their mission in this lifetime is to retain a sense of who they really are, an embodied Spirit on a mission of evolving itself, with the help of all in their chosen surroundings, animal (including the human animal), vegetable and mineral, and in turn by their own life embellishing the lives of others. Cancer is never the enemy and always the messenger.

Always listen to the messenger, especially with an open mind. Never ignore the message with criticism. Accept the message as a hypothesis and note the message any illness carries is but the introduction to the greater message to come. Illness is a wonderful ally if used as such, and should be embraced as such. It can take you on such a wonderful journey if only you have the eyes to see it spiritually.

Condensations of Spiritual Wisdom.

THE SPIRIT WORLD.

We wish to attempt to describe this world to you. We have once before described this world as a world of what you would term fantasy. Many of your writers have had to ascend into the world of fantasy in order to create a picture that represents Utopia. The degree of perfection that can be envisaged by this practice is unbelievable. You see, we are already into the concept that the conditions you will encounter here are very difficult to believe. We have also said that belief is only a part of the way to the truth. For you to experience of this truth will necessitate you totally entering this world. We have suggested that meditation it a good way of reaching the doorway into this realm.

You will have read that Jesus would lead his disciples into the Kingdom and how they experienced the ecstasy of that encounter. That Jesus brought them to the doorway in meditation and enabled them to glimpse into this world and to get a taste of the happiness and joy that exists here. You also can have that experience. You can also have the experience of meeting those whom you loved when they were sharing your world with you. Naturally you cannot stay here for any length of time because you have to complete your life there first, but it is nice to know that

75

this world is here for you to return to. People who practice meditation and gain a greater experience will describe it as returning home.

This is indeed what it is. This is the home of your immortal self, the home of your Spirit. You might ask what we do all day. We do not have day; we do not have night. What we have is continuous happiness. To help you understand we would like to compare your daily existence with our life here. When you have a good day and are happily enjoying yourself you will wish the day never ends. We see you getting tired but you still persist in getting the last ounce of enjoyment out of the day. You use stimulants in order to sustain your energy levels and thus stretch your limits. We have no tiredness and our day never ends. We have boundless energy. We have an uncluttered imagination. We can create our world to enable us to continue our happy pursuits. We have a greater clarity as to satisfying our needs. We know that we have survived death (often our greatest mortal fear). Are you getting an idea of our world?

We want to share this happiness with you but if you reject our suggestions as being too fantastic then you cannot share. Fantasy is easy to destroy. You just stop believing and it's gone. This is why there are more pessimistic people. This is why there so many depressed people. They suffer the sense of hopelessness that is fuelled by the lack of fantasy.

Children see so many possibilities for their own futures provided they are allowed by the adult to fantasise. How often their dreams are crushed by the disillusioned adult telling them that the fantasy they are engaged in is not part of the real world. Yet the world we live in is the real world and is a world of fantasy. Is it not possible that the child has a greater sense of the real world and that the adult can learn to seek the potentials that the child's fantasy can expose the adult to? It's the adult who is losing out and who is showing their ignorance by not sharing in the child's gift.

The child soon stops dreaming and the illusion turns into disillusion. The child grows into the depressed adult with no hope of living, only the hope of surviving, it's potential to create a happy life destroyed. Think of this. Allow yourself to seek the dream that can make you happy. Allow yourself to fantasise. It is a wonderful place to be and a very spiritual place to be - provided you invite us into your thoughts. We can then share our views of the life we have. Remember to us the real life is here in this fantasy land and this world is no illusion except to those who refuse to acknowledge that there is a kind loving God who as the creator of everything has prepared this world of continuance so that we may be eternally happy. Go rest in His Love and dream on.

Condensations of Spiritual Wisdom.

SOUL AND SPIRIT.

Though 'uncle George' might be 'deceased', while he is 'uncle George' he is held in soul consciousness and not in Spirit consciousness. Few appear to appreciate the difference between soul and Spirit and until this difference is recognised mediums cannot be sure what they are dealing with. Spiritualism has become psychism and thanks to the proliferation of psychics misunderstanding their role they serve the ego rather than Spirit.

Many so-called spiritual teachers regurgitate the misinformation they have been fed by their tutors without ever having questioned it. This means that the education on spirituality is not developing nor dynamic or beneficial. Too much of your understanding is based on established religions, which in themselves were developed to control the masses through the fears expounded by these religions. Look at how the threat of Karma is used to take advantage of one over the other.

One can never teach spirituality, one can only share their spiritual experiences so that the pupil can recognise and personalise their own spiritual experiences and grow in awareness and add their spiritual perspectives into the collective consciousness, and personifying their personal spiritual truth. Then they can become true workers for Spirit but only if they let Spirit direct them to the work Spirit might require them to do.

Soul consciousness is what keeps the soul restricted to 7 levels. When the soul has achieved this level, the spiritual level, it will have hopefully integrated with the positive benefits of its earth incarnation. If it has, then the Spirit can shed its soul garment and fully enter into its true Spirit state and into the Spirit World. This is why it is suggested it is important to understand the difference between soul and Spirit, Spiritualism and psychism.

ILLNESS AND SPIRITUAL HEALING.

God will always help us, often through us helping ourselves. Spiritually we are responsible but this spiritual responsibility is too often overridden by our ego. Our ego had made us ill or illness has occurred through our ego, ofttimes due to the best intentions of others or at other times through the bad intentions of others. In the latter situation the illness will highlight the weakness in the body/soul being that needs to be addressed. Somewhere within our being we have made a choice, consciously or unconsciously, to live in a particular way.

Illness gives us a clue as to the choice and validity of that choice. Our Spirit will request of God, if it doesn't already have a solution, for help in understanding the need for and cause of the illness and this understanding will be transferred to the body and healing can take place. Because so many live in the vacuum of spiritual unawareness there is a need for a physical being to channel God into that vacuum. That physical being has to be spiritually aware before an adequate channel can be provided.

That spiritually aware physical being is known as a Spiritual Healer.

Spiritual Healer, no other title will suffice, not Energy Healer, Reiki Healer, Bio Energy Healer, Angel Healer, and etc. All these other healing modalities have their place but none are Spiritual Healing. All healing comes from God but only if you ask. If you don't know God how can you ask? You can ask someone who knows God and that is a Spiritual Healer.

CHANGING.

How can one describe something that exceeds the capacity of human imagination? Perhaps it is sufficient if one were to simply label it. Why not just call it God? Should we do this then we are only limited by our imagination. Our imagination in reality is only limited by imposed and accepted parameters and the limitations of our "normal" senses. If we can't see, touch and feel something we tend to dismiss the potential of its existence. This is why there is often a reference to the "sixth sense". However, there is no such sense but there are dimensions of our existing senses that we have not accessed for many generations of human existence.

Of course there is a reason for this but unfortunately this reason is often used as an excuse, "after all we are only human". I don't think that any other creature in existence uses itself as an excuse for its limitations. Everything in creation is constantly adapting to its evolved function and governed by the one "law", "The Law of Cause and Effect", the law of constant creation. We as Spirit were indeed also created by this law.

Again, the capacity and limitations of our imagination need to be considered and by removing the limitations allow our imagination to expand. Belief is part of this process as is the ability to hypothesise, to suppose. Of course, we are confined to a certain extent by our culture and particularly by our education. These days we try and pigeon hole everything. We label and file all information. We diagnose illness by applying a list of labels that we label symptoms and forget that we are only looking at half the story. We then set about relieving the symptoms and seldom address the cause of the illness. We only try and mitigate the effect. This type of action is in fact only a reaction, a human characteristic.

In other areas of life, we also merely react. If we return to the Law of Cause and Effect we enter into the concept of "just is". "Just is" certainly requires an expanded imagination, we ask ourselves how things could possibly be the way they are. This is also when we use supposition to try and solve our dilemma. Supposition or hypothesis only opens the door through the limitations of our imagination and into expanded consciousness.

Let us then suppose that there is an existence beyond our limited consciousness. Let us suppose there is a God that defies our ability to describe. Let us suppose that that various dilemmas that occur in our lives are created through our lack of awareness and furthered by incorrect education and religious beliefs. Let us suppose that we can change our lives by creating a new attitude unique to ourselves, unique as our Spirit is unique. Let us suppose that essentially a Spirit that knows its direction of travel and also knows it is creating its own unique destination at the other "end" of eternity.

In the meantime, let us suppose that everything currently in our life has been created through our own thought and action, that everything is exactly as it can be. Let us suppose that we have the power to change all this. Then just do it.

Condensations of Spiritual Wisdom.

TITLE.

Why would anyone seek to call themselves a medium, spiritual healer, a Reiki master, a guru, a psychic, a tarot reader, an angel reader, a shaman or any such title? These are only titles that can be conferred, that can only be earned and can only be correctly used by the unaware. These are not really titles but adverbs referring to what an individual appear to be doing. Spiritually there is no right or wrong. Spiritually there is no good or bad. Spiritually everyone is doing their best. Spiritually everyone is endeavouring to do better. Spiritually everyone is seeking to grow in awareness. Physically everybody is trying to survive. If the foregoing hypothesis is correct then the question needs to be asked, "What's it all about"? But then that is what life is about, questions and answers.

The first paragraph of this dissertation raised a question, unconsciously our mind answered it. It could be said that our unconscious is our reactive, ill-informed mind, our survival mind. Our unconscious mind is always in a state of alertness to protect itself, to protect its ego. This aspect of our mind is geared to answer, not to question. This aspect is where we process what we unconsciously perceive as threats to our ignorant perceptions of who we are, a body with a Spirit. The body sees itself as the most important aspect of this human being.

The body fears defeat, fears dying, fears hurt, fears true humility. It seeks recognition and status. Spiritual awareness poses a threat as it defeats these fears but unaccountably, un-quantifiably and un-intellectually. This would therefore pose the hypothesis that the unconscious sees Spiritual awareness in opposition to ego. Where does the notion to blame, or criticise, or demean come from? It comes from the unconscious.

Continuing with the foregoing hypothesis we can see that the ego mind, the unconsciousness mind will seek to impose itself whenever it sees itself as being under threat. It will create a conflict that it knows must be on its terms and one that it will win. If it sees truth it will denounce it as a lie. If it sees or perceives higher status it will seek to demean it, to reduce that status to the level of its own, or lower. It is here that we find good and bad, right or wrong. It is here where there is very little equal or the acceptance of difference. It is here where the need for title emerges, the need for recognition occurs.

WHAT IS SPIRITUALITY?

What do you think spirituality is? My guidance on this, and I totally accept this, is that the soul is mortal and attached to the ego. Its purpose is to protect the Spirit from the negative encounters of the ego. The Spirit can have no contact with negativity in any way. Though our physical body dies the ego can still remain, energised by those in this physical world who have a memory of it. Some of these memories might be negative and these will energise the negative aspects of the ego/soul that has survived the physical passing. Of course, there are also the positive memories that retain the physical form in a soul state through the love memories. When this state is no longer required by the Spirit it is shed by the Spirit and the Spirit returns to unity with God.

Much confusion exists about these terms as religions have created a scenario to suit themselves and to enable them to maintain control over their followers. It is time now to clarify what spirituality is and to recover it from the shackles of orthodox religions. Spirituality is more than ego enhancing courses and exercises. Spirituality is about evolving truth. That's my experience after 70+ years of Cause and Effect, and working with Spirit. And that's why I asked you the question. Much love.

ANGELS.

Unfortunately, the role of Angel or God's messenger has been high jacked and almost is now a cult. As you are aware angels have no wings, nor gender. Indeed, they have no name, nor status. The hierarchy of angels was created in the 6th century by a Syrian monk and the rest as they say is history. In essence we are all, if spiritually aware and living that awareness, Divine beings and therefore carriers of God's message to the unaware. In other words, we are angels.

If God is the Christ then Christianity is the anti-Christ. Christianity has created around a human called Jesus, and deified this human by creating the trinity, thus breaking the first commandment. God cannot communicate through the closed minds of the religious. Many have also denigrated the role of angels. The 'realm of angels' was created by humankind and has now become the domain of souls who can be either "good" or "bad". Angels can no longer be trusted especially the way they are being used by many people, the same way as many psychics are ego feeders and grazers.

There is never a need for angels if one is prepared to accept their own Divinity and take responsibility for being themselves. My apologies for this long dissertation but I feel change needs to take place, and for us to see we are handing responsibility for our behaviour and life to what are lowly souls under the guise of being Spirit. My communicator wrote once, "we are not angels only Spirits".

EVIL.

No evil exists within the Spirit world. Everything that exists in your world also exists here – but in Spirit form. You might ask then if there is evil in your world then why is there no evil in Spirit. Let me explain. God is the creator of everything therefore everything must be good – of God. The world you live in, the planet you live on, everything in some way or other is God created. Even the minds of humankind, the personalities, the cultures, all God created. There are things in your world that suit certain human types yet do not suit other human types. This does not say that these things are good or bad, positive or negative, good or evil. It just means that somethings suit some people and don't suit others. The fact that they don't suit only means they must not be used by those they don't suit, not that they are bad. Some people suit other people and not others. They're not good or bad just suitable or unsuitable.

The negativity that you call evil and we call ignorance is the difference between your understanding and working with suitability and the total rejection of the "unsuitable" as being bad for all and not possibly suitable for some other. Now you know why we call it your ignorance – you didn't know that it was just unsuitable for you.

You have free will, God given to your Spirit. The free will generally exercised by you is that practiced by your human mortal mind and body in its dominance over the more subtle being – your Spirit. Your Spirit, as part of God, is also all knowing but not necessarily capable of trusting its own knowing. This is why it chooses to incarnate so that it may challenge itself, until it develops the trust in itself, that permits it to realise that it is indeed a part of God no matter how small that part may be. There is such a thing as excessive humility. In this situation the small part of God Spirit is not functioning to its purpose and in its apparent humility will not fulfil its role in God. It is not recognising its power. The challenges it experiences whilst incarnate are so that it can realise its power and practice in its entirety. Part of the errors it makes is to subjugate itself to its ego. In this state it will find a need to protect itself from the challenges that it presents itself using the tools of apathy, judgement of others, blame, conceit, self-illusion and suicide. In this process it is common to find the term evil, and if evil has to exist as the opposite to good to satisfy the human mind there must be a god of evil. Some have named this god Satan.

Evil then has been created by humankind to satisfy its own ends and to protect its ego. That is why it only exists in your world because it is created through your own ego. If you knew better it would not exist.

Evil also exists wherever there are Spirits still encased in a soul form, in other words still connected with matter, still ignorant. Their physical body has ceased to exist yet they do not possess the knowledge that can release them from the necessity to still have a body. They cannot enter the Spirit world so they occupy a space that could be deemed an in between world. Some might call it purgatory. There are not all that many there. They experience life in a very uncomfortable way. It is hard to describe how it is because you do not really know the feeling they would have unless you experienced some questionable pursuits using substances that would influence you in some undesirable fashion. You would have experienced the feeling of being in your world and yet also not being in your world and both at the same time. This confusion is what causes them to cause trouble in your world, which they can easily access. They do sometimes try to access this world but do not have the awareness to do so. If they had that awareness they wouldn't be where they are.

To acknowledge hopelessness is to empower this negativity. Hopelessness cannot exist where one knows they have the power of God at their disposal. Jesus could not have cried out in despair on the cross because he would have had the knowledge of Gods power and the hope in that. The worse things got for him the more he would have become empowered.

When humankind truly understands that everything in creation is God given, and therefore good, there will no longer be a need for your world, nor for the in between states. All will continue to exist and be utilised but only when suitable.

Condensations of Spiritual Wisdom.

THE PEOPLE OF DANANN.

(This was from a Spirit communicator who talks of a lifetime experience....)

My story begins in the far-off distant past, in a time before time. It was an era of being, an era of Spirit, a time of God. What I am about to relate is unbelievable for those who try to exist in this current age. Let us call my time B.C. – Before Corruption, and the current time C.T. – Corrupted Time. The difficulties that are experienced in this C.T. are only related to the attempts one makes to return to the paradise of B.C. There are no shortcuts. The next era is to be A.C. – After Corruption. There is no returning to B.C. rather advancing to A.C. through C.T.

Let me tell you my story. This tale spans a period of time that is so long ago the concept of years is irrelevant and the only real way of understanding the timescale is by chronicling the events that took place. This then is my story..............

It was paradise, how could it be otherwise, it was a product of God the Creator and as that was perfect. Though creation continues the earth came at a time when the evolvement towards the needs of the Creator were at a stage when the cycles of development had been brought to the stage where the Creator could sit back and allow the created to perpetuate the structures that had been put in place and evolvement became self-controlled and continuous.

Everything in God is infinite. The past is infinite. My story begins in the infinities of the past, before the cosmos, before time.

Unfortunately, this story can only be told as such, a story. I do not ask you to believe me but I do ask that you take my story as a consideration in understanding your self. Accept, even hypothetically, that there is no means for us to with our limited understanding to realise what God is. There is no aspect of God that evident in your consciousness that would in any way give you the facility to put some form that would give you the slightest idea of the true form of God. There is one exception, when you have your prayers answered in a manner that defies rational explanation, then you know God is manifesting in your life – hypothetically.

In that infinity of the past dwelt the true form of God. As we cannot understand the form of God there can be no answer to the question of the origins of God. God knew that the future was infinite and the only way that future could exist was through growth. If we apply the rule of infinites, we see that everything has infinite possibilities and this also was the task that God undertook, to create a system that could fill that future. So that this could work God began by creating the universe. This was not an easy task. The idea that everything must grow towards God and the thus allow God to grow while still respecting the nature of its self was a major challenge. It took aeons for the process to grow.

You are aware of the time it takes for a seed to grow and how you do not really know how it will develop until it completes its cycle. It might not be the expected colour, shape or size you expected; however, you will use this flower to progress to the next stage of development. This is how God worked. God developed the solar systems and all that made up the Universe but in a very unique was. It provided everything that God had created the opportunity to continuously develop itself. Throughout the Universe there are countless developments taking place continuously all related to God. We need to concern ourselves with the development we are involved in and that will better our understanding of the purpose of life as we know it and the true meaning of life. If we understand this we can evolve faster until we eventually reunite with God. This can only happen when we fully understand God and through our awareness see our place within the complexity of that form.

God created the Earth – eventually. It was created to enable the next phase of development. When I talk of development, I refer of course to the development of the immortal aspect of everything, in other words it's Spirit. God is The Spirit. Everything produced through the creative abilities of God contains an aspect of that Spirit. It is this aspect then that is developing. How that aspect is housed is as appropriate to its needs for its development. Some aspects are housed in trees, some in stones, some in insect form, some in reptile form, some in soil form, some in bird form, some in plant form, some even in animal form. You come into the latter, the human animal form. Everywhere you look, everything you see contains that aspect of God we call spirit. The responsibility to evolve gets greater the further you progress along the evolutionary chain. Choice and free will take on a greater importance in development. When you look upon this world you have participated in developing you must feel sad, it is such a mess. In the beginning of this, Earth was Paradise.

It was a world created through the perfection that existed at that time. The Earth grew into a greater garden with time. Each phase of growth showing that perfection was also part of the rule of infinity by becoming more perfect. Various species evolved through time. This development can be monitored by the various fossils that are continuously being uncovered by people who dig into the past.

WAR.

A friend sent me the following questions by text to my mobile phone and I replied also using text.

Q. Brendan is this war set in stone? How can we help the Spirit World about it?

A. Remember, nothing is absolutely right or wrong. Anything can be right if the individual chooses it to be. Therefore, for the positive purpose of war to be achieved one needs to personally form their own opinion and act upon it' taking all responsibility for their own actions. The Law of Cause and effect cannot be avoided and all are subject to this law.

Q. O.K. But is it ignorance of cause and effect or just plain hate that keeps the world as it is? Surely Guides want us to send Light to avert it for the children's sake?

A. This world is peopled by incarnate Spirits seeking enlightenment. The drama that unfolds, and includes all, is for the education of people to the Law of Cause and Effect. Inevitably all will learn but in their own time. The degree of pain suffered in the process indicates the level of ignorance that needs to be overcome. All have a part in the drama including you and I. The questions you raise and the answers given in response add to the awareness of Universal Consciousness. Maybe it is your job to raise the questions! God Bless you.

Q. How are you dealing with it in your mind? Is it imperative to stay positive no matter what?

A. By your consciousness, and the awareness of this consciousness through your feelings, you bring into this world the awareness that Spirit would require. You also contribute to the positive mass consciousness of humankind. All you need to do is be you, the wonderful Spirit Being incarnate.

THE PERSONAL POWER OF SPIRITUALITY.

The word "spirituality" is often misunderstood. Many believe spirituality is associated with religion or religious beliefs, which is partly true. Religion is about being spiritual, however being spiritual is not necessarily about being religious.

Spirituality relates to the Spirit as opposed to matter. The Spirit is the vital essence of a person. So, it can be said, that spirit and spirituality are concerning the personal and essential reasons for being incarnate, (for a Spirit to be in a body.)

Mankind, even before the oldest of today's religions began, could be considered spiritual because of their understanding and acceptance of God (The Great Spirit) in their lives. This is evidenced by the many discovered pre-historic depictions of Spirits and a divine force. Perhaps spirituality is the degree of awareness of The Great Spirit (GOD), and acting within that awareness is to be spiritual, no matter to what degree.

The essential awareness of spirit does not necessitate belonging to a particular faith, such as Christian, Muslim, Hindu, or Jew. Every prophet/founder of a religion, in their basic philosophy, agreed that re-unification with the Spirit was the goal for mankind to attain. They all taught God consciousness. However, in each case these teachers found themselves raised into the position of God by their followers. For example, Jesus who proclaimed he was the "son of man" was re-labelled - after his death - "the Son of God", and was thus deified. In short, organised religion only provides the opportunity of consciousness of its deified founder. Therefore, mankind's salvation is dependent upon the personality a particular religion sees as God. The sight of God is lost in the shadow of the prophet.

Organised religion preaches the necessity of a belief in faith. In fact, spirituality is about knowing and has little to do with belief. Belief is a transient state; that should only be occupied by those who recognise the quest they are embarking upon, the quest of knowledge and of integration with the truth. Knowing is the truth. In order to be truly spiritual, it is necessary that knowing is the goal, and not belief.

Many find themselves struggling with their beliefs, and find the limitations of accepted orthodoxy prevents them finding peace and harmony in their lives. Often beliefs are controlled by the structure that is based on the fear of God. When it is discovered there is a alternative hypothesis or philosophy outside of these limitations, allowing freedom to think and experience; allowing choice - it is an opportunity often grabbed. This theoretical philosophy can be tested; and through practice, truth in one's self can be discovered and personal power realised. Organised religion feeds on the personal power of its followers; using the fear of the wrath of God, the threat of hells fires, bad karma, etc., so as to ensure the devotees submission to the dictates of the religion. Fear empowers that which is feared: this fear allows religion to control in the name of the feared God.

The uniqueness of the self can be discovered through knowing who one is. Self-knowing can only be achieved through freedom to realise one's personal power; free from an imposed external belief system. Awareness can free the Spirit, that is the animator of mankind, into the pastures of free spirituality. Free to expand into the greatest degree of God consciousness. Free to be fulfilled spiritually. A Spirit free to fulfil its chosen Karma. If there is no awareness, that individual power and spiritual freedom can be achieved, then one will remain trapped in the ignorance of unawareness, a victim of the "mysteries".

Condensations of Spiritual Wisdom.

THE SOUL.

Every part of creation has a function that is based within Divine reason. Everything has a purpose. Look at nature where there is great order with everything working in harmony, except for humankind. (For some good reason humankind fails to see its part in creation and is the only animal that causes such disruption). This is especially true for the human species that is white skinned. The soul plays a very special part in the relationship between body and Spirit. It has been described as being an overall that covers and protects the Spirit from the difficulties that are created by the body. All the negativity that the body picks up is contained in the soul, all the positivity passes through the soul and on to the Spirit. The soul also has a means of cleansing itself.

While the body is under stress from disharmony it constantly places the soul in a negative state. Unless the body realises that it is, first and foremost, only a host for the spirit to evolve through; that it is mortal and will cease to live after it has fulfilled its purpose of hosting the Spirit, or if the Spirit sees no benefit in continuing with the current incarnation it will continue to try and take the path it sees for itself and not the path the Spirit requires.

When the body is in harmony with the needs of the Spirit, earth life flows smoothly. If there are difficulties along the way the body will not be as troubled by them as the Spirit will help overcome them. No stress is then taken on and the soul is unsullied.

THE SPIRIT.

The Spirit on the other hand is a separate entity. The Spirit is a component of God. It is of God but not God. In human terms it could be analogised as a molecule of the composition of Spirit, the composition that is called God. As in the body, each molecule has a particular and definite function, so too with God, each molecule has a particular and definite function.

This Spirit that is included in the human being is immortal; always was and always will be. It is the animator of the human form and connected to the human form through the mind. The Spirit that is part of the human being is not the total individual Spirit that is a component of God; it is a component of the individual Spirit. Humankind cannot have an acceptable concept of what God is or how vast God is. Humankind cannot have an acceptable concept of how many individual Spirit components make up God nor have an idea of how many components of the mass that occupies the human form make up the individual Spirit.

It is impossible for the human intelligence to understand the purpose of the Spirit for the time it is incarnate. The Spirit lives in a timeframe that is infinite and measures its journey through infinity be events that occur along the way. This journey is regulated by the law of cause and effect. The Spirit constantly lives in the now and everything is seen as just being. The Spirit has no expectations or demands. The Spirit sees its infinite life as a constant unfolding, dealing with the now and evaluating the results so the next 'now' can happen, whether in this world or some other world.

The incarnating Spirit chooses every journey in the physical world very carefully for the potential that the physical journey can have to encounter very particular experiences. It could be seen that the world as humankind knows it has been transformed into a material world rather than a physical world, though it is still a human made world nonetheless. Spirit will still have chosen the world as it is for its purpose and humankind in its naivety is unaware of this. Humankind thinks the world is for its existence.

THE BODY.

The body is a product of creation. Everything in creation has a particular function and that is to provide the incarnate spirit with the opportunity to achieve it purpose for incarnating. If one were to choose a particular mode of transport to take it from A to B it would select the form carefully in order to get to its destination completely. In the course of this journey, it might experience unexpected delays, breakdowns, diversions, lack of fuel. There are many events that can occur that are unplanned. The human will generally find these events a nuisance and might even choose to abandon the journey altogether. This human who terminates their journey is unaware that the journey is not for them but for their animator, their spirit. The Spirit will always accept things the way they are and will look to sees where this part of the journey has taken them to and where the next place is to be. The body's life is measured in time. Nature has provided the time clock of day and night and the seasons. Nature also shows what the right time is for everything. Trial and error will show how the assessment of the right time is correct. Do it and if it works to your satisfaction then its right for you. If it isn't to your satisfaction then it's not right for you. It's simple but requires you to take a certain risk and certainly responsibility.

But let us not feel that CREATION centres solely on God creating humankind. All has been created by God. Anything that has been created by anything or anybody or any Spirit, is imbued with the energy of its creator. A typical example would be the handcrafted object compared with the machine-made object. Why is the handcrafted object preferable? Because it is imbued with the energy of it maker! Everything in the universe was and is still being created by God in some way. If God is to inspire someone to invent something then that invention is filled with a component (Spirit) of the inventor, ('I put everything I had into inventing that'), and the Spirit of the inventor is a component of God, and so the chain goes on. Everything in the universe therefore carries a component of God, as all is of God's creation. If it can be realised that this is the case, and recognisable through awareness, then we can see God exists in everything. It is possible to see God everywhere, in everything, including in each other. Namaste, a beautiful greeting from India meaning, "That which is of God in me greets that which is of God in you."

When one can reach that stage of awareness they have finally arrived at the stage in their spiritual evolution where they can experience true peace, love and harmony. Also, at this point can unconditional love be truly practiced. LOVE is an emotion but not as would or could be practiced. Love is divine and can only be used on a spiritual level and can only be expressed through the Spirit portion of the incarnate being. If the incarnate being is dominated by the physical being this love cannot occur. It might be said that one person loves another but what is usually the case is that one body is attracted to the other body. When one has an attraction of such intensity then it is perhaps a soul-to-soul attraction but still not love.

In these two examples we look at two of the elements of the human being. The soul under these circumstances experiences the feelings of the Spirit and the body which pass through it in either direction. The body reacts within its awareness and the Spirit acts within its purpose. The body, if in the dominant role cannot practice true love as it cannot act unconditionally. The physical being, unless spiritually aware, can only respond in a reactive way whereas the Spirit can only act out the role of it purpose for incarnation.

The spiritually aware and spiritually dominant being can know and express love. Their life will be action not reaction. When the soul is included in this it can be easier to understand how conflict can occur. The soul has no function in any decision-making process. It only forms part of the trio comprising the human being. All information flows each way through it. The soul can only capture negativity and therefore when the information flow is from the Spirit there is no residue. When the flow is from the physical all negativity is filtered out of the transmission and only positivity allowed through. The residue from the negativity remains enmeshed in the soul awaiting cleansing.

The term love is most commonly used out of true context and often in the same way that other divine expressions are in appropriately used. Love is the expression of the Divine flow, is always unconditional and carries no negativity. Love is impossible to define as is God. The expression Namaste is really so appropriate, provided it is truly felt. This is definitely something for every human to aspire to.

113

PHYSICAL BEINGS.

Physical beings relate to physical things. To the human in physical awareness tangibility is generally required. It is important that any event in the human life can be related to their consciousness through one of the five senses. If one is lacking in, or partially lacking in a sense then they feel disabled. For example, if one cannot see then they are classed as blind and impaired. This applies to all the other senses. If one is lacking in an awareness of their own essence, their Spirit, it can be said that they are spiritually impaired.

The Spirit is not tangible to what might be called the normal senses. This lacking of tangibility can very often become evident by the inability of the individual to behave in an acceptable manner, spiritually. Spirituality expresses itself in a sense of knowing. The five senses that are known to humankind are taste, smell, hearing, sight and touch. Knowing is not listed. Look at how often knowing plays a part in the human life. Sometimes it might be referred to as intuition. Sometimes it is referred to as a feeling somewhere in the physical being. Usually, the feeling is physically undefinable. It might be questioned where this feeling comes from and what it is called. 'A knowing' perhaps is an adequate label to put on it. All animal forms have this knowing. Most animals act on it. The human animal often chooses to ignore it as it is intangible. This knowing comes from the Spirit that is incarnate in the human and can help give prior warning of the possible effect a particular cause might bring about. The human can feel happy or sad with the choices they might make. These are the feeling the knowing can provide, if the Spirit is addressed. God gave us these feeling to help guide us on the path of purpose.

It is the choice of the individual that brings happiness or unhappiness in to its life. If the individual can take responsibility for their own choices then they can also take responsibility for outcome of those choices. If responsibility is taken then the knowing is endorsed and the individual awareness increased, and the spirit can take another step along the path of its evolution in its present incarnation.

AWARENESS.

Awareness removes all excuses for doing wrong! Knowing is part of awareness. Awareness provides the link for all understanding of all things. The journey through spiritual growth relates to the gathering of awareness and as that awareness increases so too the confirmation that the Spirit is all knowing, always was and always will be all knowing.

Everything is right, no matter how wrong it might appear. The law of cause and effect need to be constantly recognised in order to understand this statement. If wrong is done then it needs to be shown to be wrong in order to confirm that the experience was appropriate for a learning to be gained. The law of cause and effect permits a backlash of some sort to occur that usually is unpleasant for the perpetrator of the wrong deed and they learn my accepting this was the consequences of the wrong they performed. There is no escape from this law. It is important to constantly study the law of cause and effect. It is also possible to learn that good deeds also carry pleasant experiences in the effect they can have for the person who performs them.

The Spirit is all knowing, it knows its function as part of The Spirit, God. God is constantly evolving as Its components the Spirit of everything, including that incarnate in the human form, is evolving. Nothing is finite, everything is infinite and thus its evolution draws it along the expanding path of spiritual consciousness. The law of cause and effect is the physics of this evolution.

There is talk of the end of the world and how finite that act would be. There is no end and will never be an end. Humankind looks back at its past and sees that things are different than they used to be. Some things that were appear to longer be, but that is a misunderstanding. Yes, things have changed, they haven't gone. A seed is planted in the ground and disappears only to be replaced by a plant growing in its place. After a while the plant goes through its cycle of life, providing oxygen, beauty, sometimes nourishment for humankind, sheds its leaves and gives itself back to the earth to provide a place for its own seeds to fall on and grow.

The next generation of seeds might grow in a different way than their parent as the conditions provided for their growth have changed. The plant can be said to have evolved due to the changing conditions. There is no end only change. This is not change but evolution. This is awareness. This is due to cause and effect. God planted the original seed so long ago, before time, what can be seen now is where the Spirit that is incarnate has arrived at.

LIGHT AND DARK.

There is no "dark side" in the Spirit world. There is no "light side" in the Spirit world. There are, however, many levels of consciousness, some of which have such low levels of awareness, that they might be represented as denser or dark or even perceived as evil. Evil does not exist as a state. Evil is but a human perception usually used by religions to frighten followers into the control of the church.

God consciousness does not need evil or what is sometimes referred to as negativity, to empower an awareness of its positivity. That is a human trait and not relevant in spiritual terms. When a being is in a God conscious state then it cannot be affected by any "darkness". When the Spirit is incarnate it is in a dual state of awareness, its ego and its Spirit. As the Spirit, in order to function in the earth, has to have a body, an ego, it is vulnerable to the whims of the ego. More often than not the ego becomes the dominant consciousness and the Spirit subjective to it. The longer the ego awareness the more likely the body is to suffer pain and illness of all forms. This is not to be confused with illness that can bring about a spiritual experience such as death where the Spirit

119

needed to be released from the ego world. The illness that is referred to here is the one where there is much pain but is not terminal. When the sufferer finds themselves in that state, they can pray for direction to take them to a better state. Fear is often experienced by those who need change and this can cause the condition to deteriorate further rather than improve. The reluctance to change experienced by the sufferer causes the pain to increase or become prolonged. God consciousness when exercised unconditionally and with an enthusiasm for growth and development can usually move the sufferer to a state where healing, and relief from pain abides

MORE ON GOD.

If we can begin to understand what God is rather than who God is, then we can begin to understand what we are rather than who we are; a being without an ego, a Spirit, a part of God. A being can live without a human but a human cannot live without a being. Being human is just a form, an expression of an ego that has limited existence and magnitude.

The human form is dependent on the whims of a Spirit to give it animation and direction. When that form develops a personality and seeks a life not in interdependency with the Spirit it develops an ego which to some extent can be called its own anti-Christ. The dependency the Spirit has on the human form is that need to access the world of matter. The human form is controlled by desires. The Spirit triggers these desires to direct the human form. When the human becomes addicted to desires the Spirit cannot exercise control and the human becomes subservient to its wants and is uncontrolled, except by its addictions. The human is then in an ego state. It sees itself as being something rather than part of something. The energy to maintain an ego comes from the human form and is limited. The more the human thinks of itself

121

the more the drain on the limited resources of human energy. The human in an ego state will feel the desires to replenish these resources through indulging these desires and the human will eventually fall into ill health.

The Spirit has no control over the human at this stage, and the human if left to its own resources will burn out. The indicators that this process has gone awry are the symptoms of illness. If these signals are recognized and the human surrenders itself to its relationship with its Spirit then good health can be re-attained. There are situations where this does not happen. When the Spirit uses health to control the human then it is that Spirit can use illness to terminate its connection with the human. This causes the human to die.

THE HUMAN FORM.

What created a human? The desires of two humans. These desires can be inspirationally driven or ego driven. The end result is a human form. If it is the former case then the Spirit will utilize the form as a vehicle to transport it to its material destination, death of the form. The journey is seen as life by the human and karma by the Spirit. Karma is the achievement of purpose. Every step on the road of life is purposeful when the journey is Spirit directed. It is inconsequential if ego directed, inconsequential to the Spirit. However other Spirits can benefit by observing the lives of other humans and get awareness in that way. They can show their human the folly of the ego driven desire of humanity. This can cause an action to occur within the human mind and instigate change within that human and sometimes even within humanity.

Condensations of Spiritual Wisdom.

MORE ON LOVE.

How many of us use this word, love? How many of us fully understand the true meaning of the word? How many of us recognise the true feeling of love? Please don't rush to answer these questions, as it will only be your ego that rushes to reply. Your Spirit alone knows the answers, and your Spirit will tell you the answer to all these questions is, "very few". The sad fact is, since so few know the answer many never really fully experience love.

Love is the essence of God. Love is the very core of your spiritual being. Love is an energy that flows through your Divine channels. Love is unconditional. If you are not in a state of spiritual awareness you cannot experience love, you cannot express love. In the preceding chapters we said how being spiritually aware does not mean you are spiritual, similarly being aware of love does not mean you are loving nor that you are lovable. Again, let us look to our animal pets. See how they can show us what love truly is. They love us unconditionally. The human animal finds this almost impossible to offer this love.

There are no different kinds of love, only one kind, true love. Interestingly your Spirit can only express love.

When one tries to love through their ego, the ego has a tendency to sequester that love for itself, particularly if it is not feeling loved. When we look at how little we understand love, how can we expect to know the feeling of love? Often when we spiritually meditate, we experience feelings that are strange to us. Because of these feelings we are very often moved to tearfulness. These are tears of joy and happiness brought on by the experience of the Divine flow of Love, Love from God, the Spirit, to the Spirit that is the true us.

The closest we can get to that feeling through our ego is when the heart feels it. This is why the advice is often given to go with one's heart. The human has become so desensitised to the real power of love that it uses the word indiscriminately. This word carries a power that can overcome almost anything, overcome almost any resistance. Unfortunately for the desensitised it becomes a weapon to gain control over another. It can be used to lull another into a false sense of security, making them vulnerable. It is perfectly safe to be a loving human being once one knows what love is.

Once one becomes re-sensitised through spiritual awareness and practice then one can safely enjoy what love really is. It is easy to love, harder to accept love. The older one becomes the more mistrusting they become of the term love. Because they have trusted situations in which that word was used and been hurt as a consequence, they become closed to love, they feel unloved. This is only because they have not questioned themselves as we have done in the opening paragraph of this chapter. We will reiterate, true love is Divine, true love is unconditional. True love can only come through ones Spirit. If one is unaware of their Spirit then one cannot express love. All spiritual practices involve the channelling of love. Spiritual Healing for example is the channelling of Divine Love through the ego and into the Spirit. The difference between spiritual readings and psychic readings is the presence of love. The reason why one needs to love oneself is so they will not need it from others. We stress the word need. If we can make ourselves happy then we have no need to look elsewhere. In the case of love we can be full of love ourselves, full to overflowing. When we encounter another similarly overflowing with love our love blends with theirs, and we share love.

Condensations of Spiritual Wisdom.

INDIGENOUS

SPIRITUALITY.

There are so many people trying to be somebody, not realizing they are, or not happy with, who they chose to be when they selected the parents to provide them with a body and a time and place to born into. In their ignorance they seek popularity and love posing as someone else, one that gets respect. Native American people have great respect through the spiritually seeking world, and like anything that becomes popular imitations soon start to flood the market.

Unfortunately, the imitations obscure the original. With spirituality God has been obscured by the image of Jesus. In this case it was the Romans who created this falsity on order to control the masses. Many were, and still are, victims of this deceit, and feeling disillusioned seek alternative religious solace. Native American spirituality can provide this but as it belongs to another culture does not snugly fit the psyche of those of another culture.

In my case I understand that the Native Irish spirituality was lost over many millennia starting with the arrival of the Celts approx. 3500 years ago. They were our New Agers. I feel this is where the Native American spirituality is these days. Please don't let this happen, respect and preserve all indigenous spirituality.

THE CHAKRA SYSTEM.

The Chakra system is far more extensive than normally perceived. Those who work with the Meridians know just where all these points are but for the Spiritual Healer this is not necessary to know. For now, we will concern ourselves with those main and better-known energy points, the seven centres that extend from the crown to the base of the spine.

The reason why we bother ourselves with these centres is that during the course of a Spiritual Healing career these points will be frequently encountered and a little insight into how they function in Spiritual Healing might help the healer ignore the temptation to focus onto the sensations surrounding these areas. We have discussed how the body would cease to function if the flow of Divine Energy were removed from it. These Chakra points are the entry and exit points for these energies. There are many hypotheses about the mechanics of their operation. There are many hypotheses regarding their exact location in the body. There are even diverse suggestions about the colour or hue that they emit at any given time or circumstances. I will not add to these, for in this instance there is really very little relevance to this knowledge.

The real relevance is that indeed they do exist, roughly where consensus place them and roughly operate in accordance with the popular perception. It is however interesting to note how the Chakra and its suggested position on the body is related to the gland in the Endocrine System and from there to the organ that gland serves. It can be seen that as psychics tend to use only the lower three Chakras, the area of their most common ailments relate to the organs or functions of this lower part of the body. Elsewhere you will find illustrations of the Chakra System and how it interrelates to the bodily functions. You will find that as you heal the vibrations you sense very often centre on one of these points. Without much difficulty you will also be aware of the destination of that energy flow. It is felt that these Chakra points can be so sensitive as to clog up, jam open or closed or in some way inhibit normal flow or allow uncontrolled flow of the Divine Energy to or from the body. These Chakra centres are controlled by our will. We can get Spiritual Healing, leave the healing centre and the first person we encounter who has themselves a need for healing, we open the relevant Chakra and allow our healing to flow to this other person. We feel love for someone and when we encounter them, we open our heart to them, releasing our love. Sometimes when you meet somebody for the first time you get a "gut" feeling about them. You have used a Chakra, opened to this stranger, and got back the information that you have felt in your organs.

It is incredible how we as human beings are built. It is equally amazing how the design of the life support system of the Spirit is also designed. The Spirit incarnate has this link with The Spirit through the Crown Chakra, the link with God. The integrated fitness of the body, the mind and the Spirit can only come through the correct function of the Chakra System, a system that links into all aspects of our being. This is the basis of holistic healing. Holistic healing with defined direction to God is Spiritual Healing.

Condensations of Spiritual Wisdom.

SPIRIT NEVER INTERFERES.

Our Spirit never interferes in our lives, it leads a benign role in our existence on earth. For this reason, we need to be prepared to accept the consequences of our every action. Should we fail to acknowledge the presence of our Spirit within our very being we also cannot blame God or our Spirit for not letting us know the spiritual purpose of our journey. We have made the action not our Spirit. We can ask for guidance from Spirit but we still need to make the decision. We have been selected by our Spirit as the vehicle suitable for this journey, we are perfect in that. Spirit will accept all the circumstances that occur during our lifetime as appropriate. However, should our life path, as we are leading it, threaten the safety of our Spirit an event can happen in our life that will cause us to reassess our path and to make the necessary changes to it. Should this event be ignored and blame placed outside of ourselves then a more difficult event will be necessitated. There is a saying, "things only need to get as bad as they need to get" before we pay attention and the question asked, "What am I doing wrong?" In other words, we accept full responsibility for all our decisions, even to the fact that we chose to be born into this life. Our Spirit never need to provoke these

135

events as the Law of Cause and effect, (Karma), provides the necessary reaction to our action, bad gets bad back and good gets good back. There is often a problem in this, and this is our expectations, we don't expect bad back and more often than not expect greater recognition or rewards when we do good!

As has been stated our Spirit is benign and does not interfere in our lives in any way. Whether our life is good or bad it is always good for our Spirit who can only accept the positive from it. The soul however can suffer as it has gathered all the negativity and will need to correct the awareness that generated the negativity. This awareness will make it become more enlightened and the Spirit can then be released back into its proper place, a part of God.

We never die until we have completed our journey on this earth. This journey starts when our Spirit chooses our body as a suitable vehicle. This vehicle might be classed in some cases as being defective but is can still be perfect for the Spirit. When Spirit chooses the body, the body is given life. When the journey reaches its end, the Spirit will leave the body and death ensues. The opportunity at an opportune time will enable this detachment irrespective of the circumstances. Just another change.

THE BLACK AND WHITE OF ILLNESS.

There is no "dark side" in the spirit world. There is no "light side" in the Spirit world. There are however many, many levels of consciousness some of which have such low levels of awareness that they might be represented as dense or dark or even perceived as evil. Evil does not exist as a state. Evil is but a human perception usually used by religions to frighten followers into the control of the church. God consciousness does not need evil or what is sometimes referred to as negativity to empower an awareness of its positivity. That is a human trait and not relevant in Spirit terms.

When the being is in a God conscious state then it cannot be affected by any "darkness". When the Spirit is incarnate it is in a dual state of awareness, it's ego and its Spirit. As the Spirit, in order to function on the earth has to have a body, an ego, it is vulnerable to the whims of the ego. More often than not the ego becomes the dominant consciousness and the Spirit subjective to it. The longer the ego awareness is dominating the spirit the more likely the body is to suffer pain and illness of all forms.

This is not to be confused with illness that can bring about spiritual experience, such as death, where the Spirit needed to be released from the ego world. The illness that is referred to here is the one where there is much pain but not terminal. When the sufferer finds themselves in that state, they can pray for direction to take them to a better state. Fear is often experienced by those who need change and this can cause the condition to deteriorate further rather than improve. The reluctance to change experienced by the sufferer causes the pain to increase or become prolonged. God consciousness, when exercised unconditionally and with an enthusiasm for growth and development can usually move the sufferer to a state where healing, and the relief from pain abides.

MEDITATION.

In order to understand the words, we are using here I have taken a dictionary definition for the following words: -

CONTEMPLATE – To look at thoughtfully, to think about, think about profoundly and at length, have as a probable intention.

CONTEMPLATION – The action of contemplating, religious meditation, in Christian spirituality a form of prayer in which a person seeks a direct experience of the Divine.

ISM – An unspecified system, philosophy, or ideological movement

MEDITATE – To focus one's mind for a period of time for spiritual purposes or as a method of relaxation, to think carefully about something.

MEDITATION – The action or practice of meditation, a discourse expressing considered thoughts on a subject.

RELIGION – The belief in and worship of a super-human controlling power, especially a personal God or gods, a particular system of faith and worship, a pursuit or interest followed with great devotion.

SPIRIT - The non-physical part of a person which is the seat of emotions and character, this regarded as surviving after the death of the body, a supernatural being.

SPIRITUAL - Relating to or affecting the human Spirit as opposed to material or physical things.

There are many forms of meditation, associated with the many different religions and cults and pseudo-spiritual practices. Each of these will have their own rules, how to sit, how to breathe, how to think, each rule being a tool of control by the facilitator of the method of meditation. In the West we have taken a sacred practice from the East and adapted it to our own ends. We have done the same with Yoga and Reiki, (though Reiki is not really a sacred practice but a devised therapy to simulate a spiritual practice). We have even used the religion of Hinduism to provide the basis for what is often referred to as spirituality or Christian teachings to provide the foundation for our spirituality.

We have lost the understanding that would enable us to express our spirituality outwardly or inwardly. We have been disabled spiritually. It was always the way of the Roman conqueror to outlaw the culture of the conquered and replace it with that of Rome. When Rome became Christian through the manipulation of Constantine in his seeking to become Emperor, Christianity was used and abused by Rome to impose a controllable culture on those who were to become its subjects. We are still struggling with this control, often too afraid to act outside of it. For over 2000 years we have been caught in this suppression, so many years that we are finding it difficult to move out from under the confines this imposes on us. We no longer know what else there is. We no longer know where to go. We look to other cultures and religious practices to guide us, but they too over time have been sullied by their misuse. We no longer know how to refer to ourselves. When we are asked what religion we are, we search through known religions to try and identify who we are. Spirituality is not a religion nor is any religion spiritual. We can continue to practice a religion but applying the spiritual understandings that life has given us or we can choose to practice our religion and ignore our feelings of emptiness and un-fulfilment.

How do we know what is right or wrong? We always know but often seek to justify wrong by deferring to the instructions of others; a soldier excusing the killing of another with the excuse that they were acting under orders, an executioner killing a convict with the excuse that it's the law. Life on earth is governed by Divine laws but humankind has introduced its own laws and made them the sole law instead of enacting the "soul" law. Man-made laws are there to uphold the "authority" of ruler, to enable them to continue to rule. God made laws are few and simple and when applied to life enable us to be good and decent towards each other. The law of "Cause and Effect" is the overriding law and allows the Universe to exist in a harmonious fashion, each component interdependent of each and every other component. When one component moves away from its designated function the law of cause and effect returns it to it's place in the Divine order. We will soon learn that we did indeed know right from wrong. We often try to avoid our lessons by blaming others or other circumstances for our misdemeanours and resent the "punishment" we experience. Doing this we miss the benefit of the lesson we could have learned and this will lead us to the necessity of a further experience that will appear as "bad luck" or some such other excuse we seek to use in order to avoid the responsibility of our own actions, of having to tell ourselves that we knew we were doing wrong or should have known we were doing wrong. The sooner we take responsibilities for all our actions, all our decisions, the easier the lesson will be.

How then is the best way to connect with this knowing that is there in all of humanity? Firstly, by accepting the hypothesis that in essence we are a Spirit, a component of THE Spirit. As this component we have access to all that is necessary for us to know. The way to become more familiar with that Divine aspect of ourselves is through Spiritual Meditation. Spiritual Meditation is simply "parking" the body so that our Spirit can become our consciousness.

I think that meditation is part of the path but not the goal. We must clearly define our purpose for meditating. So often people use it as a means to relax and can be heard exclaim after their meditation that they found it relaxing. For these people this was their goal and having relaxed they thought they were fulfilled. There are many forms of meditation but there is only one form when it is defined as spiritual meditation. Spiritual meditation is a sacred practice and should not be used for any other reason than to allow our Spirit connect with the Spirit. In spiritual meditation we raise our consciousness to a level where we can release our spirit from our ego. To enable this to happen we need to have the intent and then find a secure place or group to work with. This can be very hard to find as so many are proclaiming that they will teach you meditation and will offer you whatever form you like. It's like offering different flavour drinks and yet in the end they all taste the same. It would appear that mindfulness is a form of Buddhist meditation and therefore not spiritual meditation but often confused with the real thing. If practiced regularly spiritual meditation can greatly assist you in finding your own personal spiritual pathway and not one determined by a so called, self-called, spiritual teacher or guidance counsellor, or guru. In time your path will become easier for you and your life will become one with your meditation. You will then have regained your spiritual consciousness in a form that you will live by. It is then that you will find it unnecessary to set time aside for meditation and should you meditate it will be so different and spiritually refreshing.

Condensations of Spiritual Wisdom.

A NOTE FROM A SPIRIT GUIDE.

Has it occurred to any one that it is the ego that is creating all their problems? There is a constant conflict of what is perceived and what is seen. To see something is to use your physical senses which are an integral part of the ego. The senses are there as a tool to be used by the physical being and this tool for physical protection. The senses have no connection with the Spirit.

Spiritually, those who rely on the physical senses are blind and deaf. This sounds rather harsh but often using these senses to define what is needed is only to rely on the material and because the spiritual is unseen the awareness of needs is exclusive to physical needs. This is why we suggest that it is the ego that creates all of the problems the human encounters.

It was never your Spirits choice that you should have a life of pain and misery. God gave you the 'gift' of pain so that you can realise that you are not in the right place doing the right thing. How many have made career choices so that they could earn money? You will say that is the reason why people work, to earn money. Some even think because they earn big salaries that they are happy. We can see the discontentment that humankind experiences in just this one aspect of their lives. The ego needs of earning big money has no relationship with the needs of the Spirit. We addressed this in a piece we wrote sometime ago under the heading of, "Is enough, enough". Your Spirit will direct you to where you need to be unless the ego takes dominance and seeks to satisfy itself. The unhappiness you suffer, the un-fulfilment you experience, are as a consequence of the ego rejecting the notion that life can be any other way. We have also said that happiness is the key. We have suggested that if it makes you happy do it, if it doesn't make you happy don't do it'. Your ego won't let you realise your unhappiness nor will it help you realise the changes that you need to make in order to become happy. Many people feel immense relief, (once that have overcome the initial shock), at losing their job. This could be a job that they were under the impression they loved as it gave them the means of a better material life. Had they looked at it from a spiritual perspective they would have realised that the life they had subjected themselves to, was a life of subservience to an employer other than God, and to fulfil a role that was not in accordance with the plan of their Spirit. You can only be happy and fulfilled working for God. You might think that God will not pay you money for the work you do for God but God can ensure you have enough income to service your needs through the work you enjoy doing. The reason you enjoy the work is because it is your vocation, the work your Spirit needs you to do and that it can evolve while you do it. A happy life needs less money. Simplicity is inexpensive. There are so many ways that your life can be spiritually improved and yet still not be devoid of certain luxury. Your life is not meant to be one of austerity, pain and suffering. There are some who would suggest that it is supposed to be that way but they are the people who would want you to be their servant, even that you should suffer their 'suffering' for them.

Be who you are, a Spirit in a body, seeking to have an incarnation with happiness and fulfilment as it modulators. Seek direction from within your being. You are not your ego. Always look to God and to that aspect of God that you truly are. God Blesses you.

Condensations of Spiritual Wisdom.

WE COME IN THE NAME
OF GOD.

This is a very interesting world you live in. It is a world of illusion and reality. Very little is as it seems and much of what you accept is delusion.

How far humankind has strayed from the creation of God. How far humankind has created an alternative world to that created by God. How far humankind has replaced God with the material world. How far humankind had moved from a world of balance and freedom to a world of dependency and strife.

This might seem strange to you but from our perspective it is a disturbing reality. We have outlined some of the conditions that you are now subject to. In the beginning it was not this way. Creation was perfect in that it provided all that the Spirit incarnate needed. I was a simple life full of the opportunities that God had provided for the Spirit to evolve through. Life has now become so complicated for you that it is almost impossible to find that simplicity again because humankind has made it so complicated

149

and confusing. It could be said that this is the state of negativity that you all live in. Negativity has become a way of life in order for you to survive. Your life is so wrapped up in 'red tape' and rules that for you to go God's way can make life very difficult for you. When everyone else is saying yes, it is very hard for you to say NO.

On this forum we monitor all that is written. We have seen the struggles you have had between the various aspects of truth and beliefs. We have seen the petty power struggles that have gone on. We have noted sides being drawn and noticed also the attempts that negativity has made to gain control of this group. We see this but we do nothing except observe. At this time, it is only necessary that we watch. We do not judge nor praise nor condemn. It is only now that we pass comment. You will know that this group is dedicated to the work of the Divine Spirit. If you respect this group for that then we will help you in any way you let us, not only within the group but also in your life outside the group. We cherish every moment of your time that you give to us. We understand how valuable your time on earth is and we do not want any of it wasted by us.

You will notice that the energy of this group is becoming stronger. This can only happen while your awareness grows. There is no measure for this growth except that you will find the process of your understanding increasing and the hypotheses presented becoming more acceptable and less challenging. You will also notice that you will feel increasingly drawn to the truth of your own understanding. This will give you a greater sense of purpose. There are some in this group who are in it for the 'wrong' reasons. We would ask these members to realise the reason why we write 'wrong' this way is because the 'wrong' is right for them to learn from. The only difficulty we have with their behaviour is that it wastes your time, this commodity that we see you hold so dear.

From time to time we will make our continuous presence felt and at other times express our opinions on what we see you doing here. We would like to point out that we do have the ability to inspire some to leave as they are not going to benefit from this work in this group, but that is not to infer that they are in any way unwelcome here or that in some way they are bad people.

Condensations of Spiritual Wisdom.

MANY YEARS BEFORE.

Many years before I began to receive the writings that are contained in the "Teachings from The Highest Source" I got this writing from the Spirit that I later named the Essence. I didn't realise the work that was to happen before my mind was capable of receiving teachings of this magnitude. I accidentally came across this piece of writing today amongst paper work that I was sorting. I had completely forgotten about it. If you like it was the start on this period of my life, really working for God and in some way explains my intolerance to so many who would seek to block this work with sill psychic games.

This is what was written in November 1989. .... There are many who will take up the task of teaching but would rather play the dumb ignorant fool. We see these with displeasure though it is their will that they exercise and this is sacred to them. .... It is only by the utmost tolerance and understanding that any cohesion can exist. It is of paramount importance that all learn that it is not for the individual to strive ahead into the obscure future unprepared and alone, a hero. No, it must be realised that the relinquishing of the will to the work of Spirit is to enlist in an army, all fighting to achieve the same goal, God. When this is understood then perhaps the greater message can be given and understood. This message contains the understanding that when this army marches it is to a definite plan and not a haphazard excursion.

The Divine Plan that unfolds will show that everything has been carefully thought out and can only be implemented by the selfless giving of the life to the work in hand, the work of God. When on this path there is no time for trips of fancy into fairy tale worlds, too much time has already been spent at doing this already. The work of God must be treated as seriously as the desire to be by Gods side, and even more seriously to be part of the Godhead.

My friend there is much that needs discussion. There is much that needs to be seen. Too many seek to cloud your vision, as before those who were of selfish ways sought to allow you only to see that which they were prepared to show you, now we will see to it that you will see all that is to be seen. We will come at another time with the universal message for the people so that they may learn the knowledge and wisdom that is to be theirs. May God offer you all blessings and may you see fit to receive them. You have our Love.

A SPIRIT.

A Spirit has no physical dimension nor form. In the consciousness that the Spirit exists in, there is no need for a body. A body would be restrictive and limiting. In this consciousness, this physical world of matter the Spirit does need the use of a body in order to access the world of humankind. Humankind has a very specific consciousness. This consciousness permits access to specific experiences. The exactness of these experiences is dependent on the human individual experiencing them. The physical compound of the individual ensures this.

If, for example, you were to wiggle your toes, think of the process that has to take place. Firstly, the thought has to occur that our toes need to wiggle. A train of events then takes place. But where is this thought generated? Yes, in your brain, but who or what triggered this thought. There had to be a trigger. Could this trigger be your Spirit? If so, could the thought be the connection between your Spirit and your body? Could the Spirit be the animator of your body? Could your Spirit be your sole (soul) animator?

In order to understand what your Spirit is you need to enter into the consciousness of being a Spirit. In order to understand what a body is we need to enter into a state of physical consciousness. When in physical consciousness, we realise that the physical world is full of physical obstacles, and we constantly need to direct ourselves around them. These obstacles can be physical or mental in nature. They only exist as obstacles in the physical sense for those that are in physical consciousness. They do not present as an obstacle to those in Spirit consciousness and without a physical body. This is why if we are to go into a deep meditative state it is possible to bi-locate. In other words, your Spirit can be in one place while your body is in another place.

Your body will always remain where your Spirit left it - unless somebody else moves it. Your body will remain alive, though inanimate, until your Spirit returns to it. In general, this is not a good practice as the body must be in a very safe place or it could be occupied by some other Spirit. This would be a typical scenario for possession.

UNDERSTANDING.

The more I develop spiritual awareness the greater my understanding of things, however the more I develop spiritually the less I understand why humankind needs to make everything so difficult. Spirituality is simplicity itself and only requires awareness to trigger spiritual growth. It does not benefit from intellectualising nor the unlocking of some great code.

It is not a secret nor the possession of any guru. It is the environment, the collection of all species and the universe itself. Everything that has been created has the imprint of its creator in it. The artists imbue themselves in their artwork, the architect in his buildings, the potter in his pots and the sculptor in his statues. Experts can look at these creations and instantly recognise the artist in the work. God, in the creation of all, imbued an aspect of God in all that God created. Everywhere you look you can see the evidence of the Creator, in the flowers, the trees, the animals, in all that is nature. What humankind fails to see, when looking at all these things is the style of the Creator and how visible it is to us all. We fail to see God in everything especially in our own kind, especially in our selves.

Again, it is simplicity. Humankind is so concerned in finding how it's is made, what is the substance of the flesh and blood and organs of the body. We want to know how it functions, how to repair it, how to keep it going. At the same time, we set out to damage it, to mistreat it, to not respect it. It is a peculiarity of humankind that when it gets something easy it disrespects it, often neglects it, as it does not appear to have a value. We only keep our bodies going so that we can continue to get around this world of ours and earn a living. Really, we do less than that. In most cases we only manage to survive.

Survive for what reason? Is it because we have a fear of dying? Is it because of the loss we feel we suffer through death? Is it that we do not know what lies ahead of us when we die? Or is it that we fear there is nothing, that death is the end. If the latter is the case then birth must be the beginning? Then the body is but a result of some biology. We know that the process that the cells go through, dividing until they eventually arrive at being a body but this is where the process makes a change. The body becomes animated. The body begins to move. The body begins to connect with the world outside the womb and eventually when the time is right it emerges out into this world of matter, a being created by a man and a woman, carrying the characteristics of both it parents. But there is something more there.

There is also the characteristics of it trues creator, the creator who devised the biology and the Creator who impressed itself on it's creation, God the Creator, God the Spirit. Spirit is the life-force of all in creation. What keeps us on the move going forward is instinct that comes from a knowledge buried deep within us. This knowledge is not gained in this lifetime but life is used to confirm we have and to apply it in a positive way. When this is achieved, we can then reunite with our nature and once again become one with God.

Condensations of Spiritual Wisdom.

Printed in Great Britain
by Amazon

79026820R00092